April 86

Amy

We will do the
town when you
get to New York

Frank & Dean

NEW YORK

Photographs by Bernard Hermann

Text by Gilbert Millstein

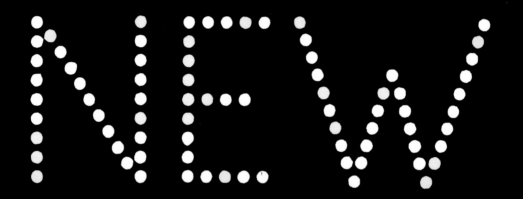

YORK

Harry N. Abrams, Inc., Publishers, New York
in cooperation with
les éditions du pacifique, Papeete, Tahiti

Library of Congress Cataloging in Publication Data

Hermann, Bernard, 1941-
    New York.

    1. New York (City)—Description
I. Millstein, Gilbert. II. Title.
F128.52.H43   917.47′104′40222   77-1860
ISBN 0-8109-1350-X
ISBN 0-8109-2071-9 pbk.

Library of Congress Catalogue Card Number: 77-1860

Published in 1977 by Harry N. Abrams, Incorporated, New York
Copyright © 1977 **les éditions du pacifique,** 10 avenue Bruat, Papeete, Tahiti
All rights of translation, adaptation and reproduction reserved for
all countries. This book was prepared by **les éditions du pacifique**
in its Cities series.

Printed and bound in Japan

CONTENTS

NEW YORK

THE GREAT
EASTERN GATEWAY

For many years now, I have returned to Manhattan from the airports—
Kennedy International, when the flight to New York was a long one; LaGuardia when the flight was much shorter—over the Brooklyn-Queens Expressway to the Williamsburg Bridge. One is apt to be tired at such times no matter
how short the flight and slightly depressed by the airline food, the pressure of
descending, the wait for baggage, the megalomania of New York City hackies
driving sixty-five miles an hour over bad roadways. Yet I am also
exhilarated—a tiny anticipatory tingle in my breast, a purling of excitement at
who knows what in my belly. I know what is there. But *what* is there?

I am driven home at breakneck speed. What sort of jazzy Grand Prix
does this mad driver have in mind as he takes our lives in his hands in and out
of the narrow pieces of road left by enormous aluminum trailer trucks,
Cadillacs, Volkswagens, the rusty heaps all going more slowly than he? And
he, all the while, chewing on a cheap cigar, unlighted, and swearing to
himself. The meter will never click fast enough for him. But, fast as he may
drive, whatever Homeric rage consumes him, whether it be day or night,
sunlight, rain, fog, the green smokes sent up by factories darkening the skies,
he cannot go so fast that I do not see that which always tells me that I am
home.

What I see to my right just before I reach the bridge had become one of
my several metaphors for New York City long before I found out anything
about it. It is a small old apartment building, its bricks painted a pale yellow,
its fussy cast-iron pilasters, sills and lintels a chocolate brown, its top story

(the third) surmounted by a tin cornice, also painted chocolate brown and of a size and elaborateness out of all proportion to the simple building beneath it. (Once, that was not uncommon, either in New York or anywhere else in America.) There are lattice ornaments at each side, separated by corbels, and, in the center, the marvel: There, framed in three swags and set out in large letters painted gold is the legend, "John Ottati 1900."

The cornice and the name speak, quite obviously, of accomplishment and of pride. That was easy enough to figure out and that was all I knew. But I decided that that was not enough and so, one hot, hazy Sunday morning, I made my way out to "John Ottati 1900" in the Williamsburg section of Brooklyn, walked up the three cement steps into the narrow vestibule and looked at the names on the doorbells. They read, "A. Indelicato," "E. and M. Murphy," "M. Parisi," "Michaud," "Staton," and "John Ottati and C. A. Santelli." My God, I thought, John Ottati still alive? I rang the bell, the buzzer let me in, and a heavyset man in his middle 40s, partly bald, appeared at the top of the first flight of stairs. I explained why I was there, which he didn't seem to think odd, but he said, not abruptly, "I can't talk to you now, I'm clocking a pigeon race." Before he disappeared into his apartment, he did say that his name was Carmine Santelli, Jr., that he was the grandson of John Ottati, and that John Ottati had been dead for forty-three years. And he said I could come back one evening the following week.

Which I did. And came to realize the richness of the metaphor which was, in fact, the recapitulation of the great immigration through the Eastern

Gateway to the United States and the rise of a poor man to an eminence which, finally, he expressed in the building which says "John Ottati 1900" on the cornice. This is some of what I learned, sitting around the dining-room table with Carmine Santelli, Jr., with his father, who is 81 and one of John Ottati's sons-in-law, and with Marie Santelli, a sister who did not marry.

John Ottati was born in Salerno, Italy, in 1857, one of three brothers. (Salerno. I was reminded, poignantly, of the allied invasion of Italy in the Second World War.) One of his brothers preceded him to the United States; the other followed. They, too, are dead. John Ottati was a constable of sorts in Salerno, hired to protect the farms and livestock and stores of his neighbors. He could not read or write and never did learn. As for all the millions who preceded him, who followed him, the pull of the United States was irresistible. Italy, under the House of Savoy, was a miserable, tendentious little monarchy; the romantic revolution of Garibaldi was over and Garibaldi dead. And so, Ottati came to America—in steerage, like most of the rest, propelled to Williamsburg, in Brooklyn, by some forgotten *padrone* looking for cheap labor.

His family told me that he was a fine-looking man, six feet three inches tall, and got out a family photograph taken at a wedding many years before to prove it. John Ottati sits at the right, splendid in a heavy, black wool suit, his derby resting on his left knee. His shoulders are very broad, his chest deep; he is too big for the chair in which he is sitting. He has a thick, curving mustache of the kind foreign men wore in those days and his hair is cut short because he had been a constable, which is a kind of military man. He is smiling faintly, in consonance with the mustache and the occasion (the wedding of a daughter)—altogether a powerful and confident man.

He did things I think were remarkable. Ottati was 27 when he got to New York City, entering through Castle Garden at The Battery; Castle Garden, once a fort guarding New York Harbor, once a concert hall in which Jenny Lind, the Swedish Nightingale, sang, then the place through which immigrants were pushed, higgledy-piggledy into America until Ellis Island opened in 1892. He became a junkman, picking up rags, bottles, anything. (Remember all the immigrant Jews making their way through the Lower East Side of Manhattan, crying up to the backyard windows of the tenements, ''I cash clothes''—buying tatters secondhand for very little and selling for just a little bit more.) Some *Salernese,* some *cumbar,* or countryman, lent John Ottati enough money to buy a horse and wagon and so, slowly, this strong, illiterate man prospered, married and had a family.

Consider the solid house he built which bears his name. John Ottati decided early that he wanted to build a house, and, being an ambitious man, it must be one in which he could live *and* rent out. In 1897, construction of the Williamsburg Bridge between Manhattan and Brooklyn began. Everything in the way of its approaches was torn down—houses, factories, the mansions of the very rich who lived in Brooklyn on the hills above the East River. First, John Ottati borrowed enough money from his compatriots—a few hundred dollars—to buy three lots. Then, day in and day out, month in and month out, he picked up bricks from buildings that had been torn down and steel girders and piled them on his weedy lots. In those days, the practice was not uncommon. Finally, when he had collected enough brick and steel, Ottati hired a contractor (on a handshake) and began to build. And, in 1900, the building was finished. The only new things in it were steel piping for the running water, lead piping for the toilets and the cornice which would memorialize John Ottati.

It has—as much as his descendants, as much as anything in his life. He lived in it until he died. His children and grandchildren were born in it; some of them, as we know, still live in it and they own the building free and clear as well as the land it stands on. And there, they told me, they intend to live for the rest of their lives, despite the noise of the expressway, whatever the deterioration and decay around them. They recall that John Ottati, whenever he went away from the house for a day or so would come back, contemplate the building, and say, "There is my palace."

So, that is the finest of the metaphors I have for New York City, the city of my birth and most of my life. I place that building in the same rank with the Statue of Liberty, the skyline seen from Brooklyn, Staten Island or New Jersey; with upper Fifth Avenue and Central Park and Greenwich Village and the noble museums and the universities and the terrible slums. There is no race on earth that has not known New York City at one time or another. I know that it has lost population and that it has declined, as old cities do everywhere in the world. Nobody has to tell me about crime or poverty or the kind of mean skulduggery in public and private places which has made life in the city pure Hell for so many people. Nor do I have to be reminded that it is still a focus of art and commerce and literature and music for all the world.

I know the city from Peter Stuyvesant and the British governor, Lord Cornbury (a scoundrel and eccentric who had the habit of parading around in women's clothes), to Mayor A. Oakey Hall and Boss Tweed; through Tammany Hall and Jimmie Walker and Fiorello LaGuardia and Abe Beame; through Astors, Vanderbilts and Belmonts; such thieves as Jay Gould and Jim Fisk; and the eternal tearing down and building up; the great accretion of learning and the arts. I sometimes think, *I shall go down with it,* and then, rationally, *I know better. It will survive me.*

Four hundred and fifty years ago or so, the explorer Verrazzano, upon sailing into New York, wrote, ''We found a very agreeable place between two small but prominent hills; between them a very wide river, deep at its mouth, flowed out into the sea.'' Poetry. He had, though not knowing it, written of the greatest harbor in the world and what was to become the great Eastern Gateway to the United States. Also, not knowing it, he had said something of what was to become and remain (even in its present decline) the greatest city in the world. I can live in no other and I want to die in no other. I am no different from John Ottati 1900.

The skyline of Lower Manhattan was transformed in a frenzy of tearing down and building up in the years following the second World War. Now, whether the skyline is seen from the air *(right)* or from the vantage point of Liberty Island *(below),* it is dominated by the 110-story towers of the World Trade Center at the left. There was a time, not that long ago, when the Moran Towing Company people would summon their tugboats in the harbor by bawling through a megaphone from a window of the building that stands in the lee of the South Tower of the Trade Center.

Edouard René de Laboulaye, a Parisian politician, writer and lover of all things American, once wrote, "The folly of love and the madness of ambition are sometimes curable, but no one was ever cured of a mania for liberty." Years later, having discussed the American Revolution and Lafayette with a group of intellectuals, he had another conversation on the subject with a young sculptor, Frédéric Auguste Bartholdi. What to give America on its centennial? "I think," Bartholdi said, "it would be well to offer the Americans a statue of liberty."

In October, 1886, Bartholdi's Statue of Liberty was erected and dedicated in New York Harbor—225 tons, 305 feet and one inch from the tip of the torch to the pedestal. It is very likely the most famous statue in the world.

All manner of movers and shakers have left marks on New York. A waterjet fountain was put at the southern tip of Roosevelt Island in the East River by the publisher, George Delacorte. Behind it, to the left, is the United Nations.

Of all the monuments seen on these pages *(left and right)*, by far the greatest, the most beautiful, is the Brooklyn Bridge—the Great Bridge, as it was known. It is the work of two Roeblings, father and son, and has inspired poetry and prose, painting and music, some of it as imperishable as the bridge itself.

The World Trade Center towers, seen from Brooklyn Heights, are the over-ambitious conception of the Port Authority of New York and New Jersey, designed by a Japanese-American architect, Minoru Yamasaki.

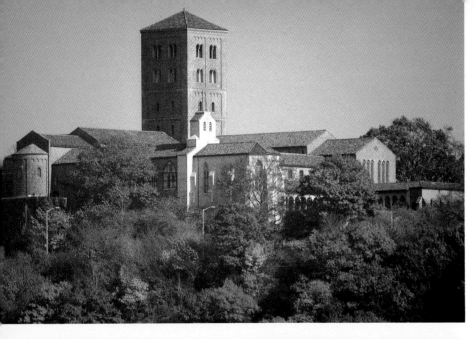

Preceding page: from the promenade on Brooklyn Heights, still another view of Lower Manhattan.

Left: The Cloisters, run by the Metropolitan Museum, a chapter house and parts of five medieval cloisters (and their furnishings) set down on a wooded hill in Upper Manhattan.

These late-Victorian frame houses stand on the bluff just across the Hudson from Manhattan in New Jersey.

For all that it has been exceeded in height by the Trade Center, the Empire State Building is still a talisman for many New Yorkers. It stands on the site once occupied by the old Waldorf-Astoria Hotel. On the following page, downtown New York, south from the Empire State Building.

Another way to see the skyline, left, is from the Staten Island Ferry. Once a nickel a ride, now a quarter, it still provides the cheapest tour of the harbor.

If New York is to be grasped at all, it is in its particularities: the gentleman with the opera hat is only the driver of an open carriage. He is parked near the Plaza Hotel waiting for customers.

The lady is expressing something, but what we cannot tell.

The police on parade duty are bored.

The Bowery bum expresses a sodden disapproval.

It is heartening to find football being played by young people amid the noise and congestion of the South Bronx. Not everything is lost there.

New York City is full of churches, and God is
pursued with surprising avidity. It may not be so
surprising, after all, though: survival is a chancy
matter in the city and one may try worship. So, we
have a Black Muslim worship service, a Chinese
Buddhist ceremony, a grave discussion outside the
door of one of the dwindling number of synagogues
on the Lower East Side of Manhattan.

I think it is curious and even faintly comic but certainly true that although the Borough of Brooklyn was incorporated into the City of New York in 1898, people who live in Brooklyn still say, when they have occasion to go to Manhattan, that they are "going into the city," or "going to New York." They state this as fact, although, of course, it is only a belief, a state of mind. But it is a belief held by almost every New Yorker and by every traveler to New York for centuries. For them, Manhattan is New York.

Such travelers include Anthony Trollope, the English writer (he was much taken by the city), his mother (she despised it), Charles Dickens (he saw powerful parallels with the underside of London) and Oscar Wilde (he was amused by it, as he was by the rest of America, more so by New York because its excesses were so very metropolitan). People are transfixed by Manhattan.

This attitude is probably best epitomized by something the English novelist and poet, Charles Kingsley, visiting New York in the last third of the 19th century, had to say. His ship was coming up the bay. A deputation from the Lotos Club, a group of earnest, sober literary and artistic lights of New York, came out to his ship on the pilot boat to invite him to a banquet. "Gentlemen," said Kingsley, all punctilio, but nevertheless determined, "I am trying to view the approaches to New York. I cannot make any engagements now."

Baroness Hyde de Neuville, in addition to the journals she kept of her stay in New York, left us a series of beautiful and delicate watercolors of 18th-century New York. A hundred or so of the baroness's drawings and paintings may be seen at The New-York Historical Society and they show us a Manhattan which has been resolutely erased by the gigantic energies of the people who have populated it: A New York of small houses in the Dutch or the Federal or the vernacular style; dusty lanes and rutted, narrow dirt roads; ladies and gentlemen and children and the coarser types in the streets, together with dogs and horses and wagons.

Much of that city, Dutch and English, was destroyed in fires, particularly the Great Fire of 1835, December 16 and 17. That fire, and its aftermath, may be seen in two prized aquatints by the Neapolitan painter Nicolino Calyo, who lived in Manhattan at the time. And they are described at great length in the diaries of Philip Hone, once the mayor of New York. At one point, Hone speaks of "the most awful calamity which has ever visited these United States . . . the greatest loss by fire that has ever been known, with the exception perhaps of the conflagration of Moscow. . . ." He says his "fancy" is "filled with images of horror which my pen is inadequate to describe." But two days later—and here is the true gauge of the New Yorker—he sets down this: "It is gratifying to witness the spirit and firmness with which the merchants meet this calamity. There is no despondency; every man is determined to go to work to redeem his loss, and all are ready to assist their more unfortunate neighbors."

If that is not entirely true today there is still enough of "spirit and firmness" to keep Manhattan and New York from going under. The building has never stopped, even now when money has moved West and South and the city is pinched. Even as the slums grow more vast, the buildings grow higher and higher (although at least one of them, a skyscraper in midtown, has no tenants at all); and a crazy profusion of plans is made, most of which will never be carried out; and some calmer heads and lovers of Manhattan work, molelike, to preserve what is left. One of the favorite banalities concerning New York says it'll be a hell of a place if they ever finish it. In her long *History of the City of New York: Its Origin, Rise and Progress,* Mrs. Martha Lamb, a hundred years into the Republic, wrote: "Various landmarks have passed away; and property has changed hands and risen in value, in a ratio, which, if fully described, would seem like the vagaries of imagination."

It seems to me that in that sentence, written a dozen years after the end of the Civil War, Mrs. Lamb expressed a kind of awe, not untinged with apprehension and anticipation, which has assailed everyone who has ever had anything to do with Manhattan. She was well aware of the technological and economic and social forces which had been let loose with the end of that war, but she could not have foreseen what was to happen after the end of another war, the Second World War, through the geometric progression of those forces.

I mark those years as the time when those "vagaries of the imagination" began to be realized. And I note the Recession of the Seventies as the time when they were, to all intents and purposes, completed and Manhattan was transformed once more—almost beyond recognition for anyone over the age of forty. I find it astonishing that buildings so young as the Empire State and the Chrysler (both in their forties) should be regarded as landmarks. But, then I am forced to remember that Cass Gilbert's Gothic Woolworth Building of 1913 was once thought of as one of the Seven Wonders of the World. And, I must reckon with the World Trade Center, with its two foreboding towers, a building for which an entire neighborhood was torn down—a neighborhood of small businesses and narrow streets near the moneymaking machinery of Wall Street and not far from the splendors of Trinity Church and St. Paul's Chapel.

Acres and acres of anonymous glass and steel and concrete structures have been put up in Lower Manhattan and up the long straight avenues of midtown. They are oppressive to many people. But, like any native New Yorker (there are fewer New Yorkers now; the population has fallen about a quarter of a million to seven and a half million), I am not without common sense and I take my consolations in many of the things around me. I will name a few.

If I am in Rockefeller Center, I may sit on a bench in the Channel Gardens leading toward the skating rink, and take in the Paul Manship statue of Prometheus with his silly, stylized flame in hand, and the 70-story tower of the RCA Building. And, if I look across Fifth Avenue, I can see St. Patrick's Cathedral, the symbol of the Roman Catholic Archdiocese of New York.

Rockefeller Center is built on land once owned by Dr. David Hosack, a graduate of Columbia University who grew medicinal herbs in his garden. (Dr. Hosack also was the physician to Alexander Hamilton and attended him in his dying hours, after he had been shot by Aaron Burr in a duel across the Hudson River in New Jersey.) Dr. Hosack left his garden to Columbia; the land still belongs to the university and not to Rockefeller Center, and, once a year, just to keep everything legal and tidy, Rockefeller Plaza is closed to traffic, a reminder that it is not a public street.

As for St. Patrick's, it is one of the monuments left behind him by James Renwick, the architect also of Grace Church. (Nothing sectarian in that man; he built for both

Catholics and Episcopalians.) St. Patrick's was proposed by Bishop John Hughes to take the place of Old St. Patrick's downtown. That was before the Civil War and people thought him mad. Who, they said, would ever attend Mass that far uptown? But Hughes persevered and Renwick built and today the Easter Parade, bright, vulgar and highly self-conscious in its publicizing of things which have nothing to do with Easter Sunday, still goes on in front of St. Patrick's. I think it noteworthy also that a block north of St. Patrick's, where Cartier, the jeweler, now occupies an old limestone town house, once stood the brownstone mansion of Madame Restell, the most notorious abortionist New York has ever known. (Her clients were the very rich; she was constantly being inveighed against from the pulpit; and she came to no good end—killed herself, in fact.)

I am alternately appalled by Times Square and still attracted by the theatres around it, even though most of them seem to have been swallowed by decay, on the one hand, and by huge, untoward skyscrapers on the other. And I still enjoy enormously walking down Fifth Avenue on a fine day. The women walk with a sprightlier step down Fifth Avenue and the men forego their grave preoccupations to speculate on them. I can buy hot dogs in the side streets off the Avenue, if I wish, or lunch in a good Italian restaurant.

And, there are other diversions. One afternoon, walking down the Avenue from Rockefeller Center, I was handed a leaflet at Forty-fifth Street. It had on its green paper a photograph of a naked young woman. The leaflet informed me that a few steps west—and for only $10—I would find "BEAUTIFUL GIRLS of All Nationalities" *and* "Complete Satisfaction" and "NO OTHER CHARGES WHATSOEVER." If I didn't understand that, the leaflet let me know about "CHICAS DE TODAS NACIONALIDADES" and "$10 NO HAY COBROS MAS DE NINGUNA CLASE." At Thirty-fifth Street, another leaflet: "$15 a complete session. A unique concept. NO TIPPING NECESSARY. NO HIDDEN CHARGES. YOUR CHOICE OF LOVELY MODELS. SAFE, CLEAN, SECURE. WE WANT YOU AS A REGULAR CUSTOMER."

A few blocks farther down, another leaflet invited me to a "Mass anti-apartheid day" at Herald Square and I could march, if I wished, to South African Airways back up the Avenue near Forty-ninth Street. More leaflets: "Wonderland Fashions Inc. Is On STRIKE" and "AWAKE! CRUELTIES GO UNCHECKED IN MALAWI. Peace-loving Christians persecuted."

I could go on and on sprinkling the earnest and the absurd of Manhattan about me, but I will content myself with one last one. Three men were arrested for running a call-girl business out of the New York City morgue. They had used the Medical Examiner's office (and telephone and automobile) the police said, to send two girls around the city to clients willing to pay as much as $250. Think of it. There they sat, those three, dispatching soiled doves to this hotel and that apartment without let or stay until an undercover policewoman got on to their dodge. I rather doubt any such thing ever happened in any other city on earth. In an oblique way, it further justifies my belief in the ability of New York City to get anything done.

New York at night. If Paris is the City of Light, then New York at night is a city in which light has been made to illuminate vistas otherwise unimaginable. The picture of the Empire State Building at the left was taken from the top of another splendid tower, the RCA Building in Rockefeller Center.

In the financial district *(left and below)*, New York renders unto Caesar the things which are Caesar's (the columned building is the New York Stock Exchange) and unto God the things which are His. And while all this is going on, the Good Humor man renders ice cream to *hoi polloi*.

Trompe l'oeil during lunch hour in the neighborhood of Rockefeller Center on Sixth Avenue. Fiorello LaGuardia renamed it The Avenue of the Americas but no one calls it that.

The dust of New York is so fine, so pervasive, that no amount of window washing will ever remove the screen it creates, but the window washing goes on, day in and day out—from the top of a building to the bottom and then from the top again.

Most of the city's skyscrapers get their steam for heating from miles and miles of underground steam pipes. The pipes are hot; the air about them rises to the street, and, lo! everyone wonders where the steam is coming from. It is only hot air condensing in the cooler air above ground.

The word ''Bowery'' in Dutch means farm, and this wide, bleak avenue once was a part of one. It is hard to believe that it was once a center of music halls and first-rate theatre. Now, it is simply the place where the bums exist—exist, not live. Any number of psychological studies have been made of the bums. They explain nothing. One thing seems to have changed among the bums in the last thirty years or so. They are younger. And, oh, yes. There are now women among them. Indistinguishable in behavior, even in dress, from men bums. It is another form of equal rights.

More vistas. On the preceding page, the wide-angle lens shows the shadow of the Empire State Building flung over midtown. The view is to the north; Central Park is hidden behind the ranks of skyscrapers.

At the left, looking south on Sixth Avenue from Central Park in early evening.

At right, a man descends out of daylight into the bowels of the New York subway system. For a single token he may ride endlessly over more than 700 miles of track.

Even though the subway system has been losing riders steadily as the fares go up and people move to the suburbs, the ride at rush hour is still a crowded one. The New York City subway system is the biggest in the world and the safest, but it is also the noisiest and the dirtiest. And nowhere else in the world is public transport decorated so effusively with graffiti. They have taken on the status of a new form—at least among a few chic thinkers.

The range of architectural styles and building decoration in the city is nearly as wide as its ethnic mix: below, at left, a Hollywood version of Moorish style. At center, the extraordinary Art Deco tower of the Chrysler building, and to its right, a stainless steel corner ornament from the same building. At the bottom of this page, a window mural on a store-front awaiting a tenant. Opposite, along West 57th Street, is the curved front of a new building designed by Gordon Bunshaft.

The Chrysler Building was
finished in 1930 and, until the
Empire State Building was
finished a few months later,
was the tallest in the world. It
is the work of an architect
named William Van Alen; it
stands at the northeast corner
of Lexington Avenue and
Forty-second Street and is probably
the most stunning example
of Art Deco building design
New York City has to offer.

Art Deco style dominates Rockefeller Center, too. We see it in the gilded Paul Manship Prometheus at the skating rink and on the buildings of the Center.

But, look across the street, through the Atlas which stands in front of another of the Rockefeller Center Buildings. And there, you will see the Gothic masterpiece of James Renwick, architect—St. Patrick's Cathedral.

On the preceding page, the wide-angle lens does something for us that a single glimpse of the eye cannot: it takes in a great deal of Rockefeller Center— Prometheus and the RCA Building, the wall of the sunken plaza, and other buildings of the Center.

One might expect birds to lose their élan in New York. But the pigeons do not. A traffic-light arm is the same to them as a tree limb.

The bastard Renaissance tower is that of the Sherry-Netherland Hotel at Fifth Avenue and 59th Street, one of the remaining aristocrats of the Avenue. The uncompromising facade behind it is that of the nearby General Motors Building. An *arriviste*.

Horse-drawn carriages wait near the hotels at Fifth Avenue and 59th Street to carry romantics (at high prices) through Central Park.

Late in the summer of 1976, the Radio City Music
Hall, without which no visit to New York was
complete, almost shut its doors. It had been losing
too much money to suit its owners. But a
compromise was arrived at with the unions. The
music is still played by the big orchestra; the
Rockettes still perform their miraculous mechanical
dances. And, across the street, the propagandist for
dissatisfied husbands still peddles his pamphlets.

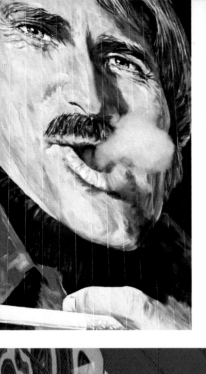

On the preceding pages and here are some of the faces of New York buildings—and the paint, steel, chrome, glass and neon that are the city's cosmetics.

Digital clocks tell the time on Times Square and signs inform us that the City was the first capital of the United States. And the horse cop tells us that whatever the city is or might be, Times Square takes a lot of patroling.

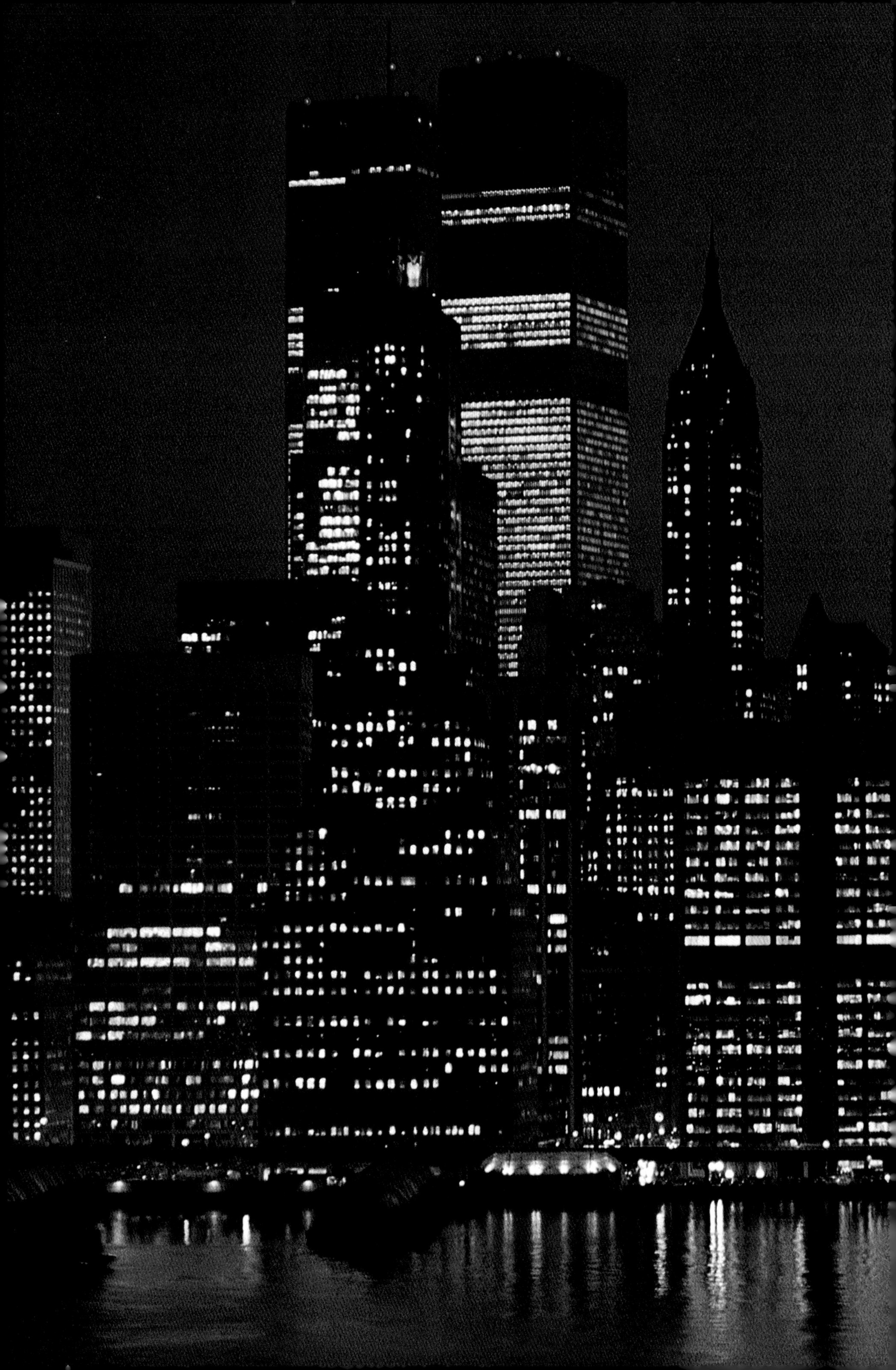

In a book called *Mental Health in the Metropolis, The Midtown Manhattan Study,* one of the authors, a psychiatrist and sociologist, wrote that he "stands neither with the advocates who find in Manhattan the penultimate stage of the heavenly city nor with those who regard it as a purview of purgatory." Which is temperate enough, by comparison with the attitude of the late Frank Lloyd Wright, the architect. "Here," Wright set down in his characteristically bravura manner, "is a volcanic crater of blind, confused human forces pushing together and grinding upon each other, moved by greed in common exploitation. This mantrap of gigantic dimensions, devouring manhood . . . is as good an example of barbarism as exists."

Nevertheless, Wright, for all of his godlike manner, permitted himself to be prevailed upon to build something in New York, a city in which, hitherto, he had built nothing. Unquestionably, he realized that New York was then—and still is—the very focus of art and music and writing and painting and of commerce and finance and communication, and that while he might make his mark in Chicago or at Taliesin in the West, he must, if the mark were to be indelible, make it in New York. And so, for all his fulminations, he gave New York the Solomon R. Guggenheim Museum of art on upper Fifth Avenue. No matter that there are those who suspect that the museum is only the emendation of plans originally made for a parking garage in Pittsburgh. No matter that the ramps from floor to roof produce vertigo and that special arrangements had to be made to angle paintings outward so that they could be seen and lighted. Wright *had* to build in New York.

Certainly, the pressures of living and working in New York are gigantic.

It could not be otherwise—any more than it could have been in Rome or Alexandria or Athens—for New York is, even now, the greatest city in the world, and, being so, the most difficult in which to live. It requires the utmost cunning to relieve oneself of its pressures. Melville, for example, hated New York (you can tell that from his peculiar short story, "Bartleby The Scrivener"), but, late in life, he could be found walking in Central Park with his granddaughter. On the other hand, E. B. White, the essayist, loved the city, but, in the end, moved away.

I can recall—vividly—a man who worked for a magazine, in whom the pressure of living in New York grew too great. One night, on deadline, he got up from his typewriter, walked over to the window (the magazine overlooked Rockefeller Plaza), opened it and looked out briefly. It was a hot, bad night, and he was behind. All the same, he straightened his tie, put on his jacket, picked up his typewriter (a heavy, standard-size one), dropped it out the window (first making certain there was no one below), walked out the door and disappeared.

I have chosen to stay. So have millions more. Still other millions, being poor, have no alternative and they stay. And all of us, each in his own way, withstand the pressure, endure the frustrations and the constant plucking at the nerves and the constant roar of the city, the screaming of a dozen different kinds of sirens. We know that we can be mugged, sometimes killed, and still we stay. We pay too much for far too little and we are governed by as outstanding a body of rascals as ever infested the earth. And still we stay. We stay because there are ways around the pressures. Some of those ways are well known to tourists, but they are our ways, too. And some are our very own.

Somewhere in New York, every day, every hour, one can do, or eat, or see, or obtain, anything. Anything at all, from the meanest to the most sublime. If I wish, I can go to Frank Lloyd Wright's Guggenheim Museum, risk dizziness on the ramp, and think about the physics of a Kandinsky painting. At the Modern, I can take my pick of Picasso's *Demoiselles d'Avignon* or go downstairs to see Eric von Stroheim's masterpiece of a movie, "Greed." (A couple of blocks to the west, around Times Square, I have my pick of other movies—pornographic ones). If I go to the Metropolitan, I may contemplate Rembrandt's *Aristotle Contemplating the Bust of Homer,* and think of how much it cost the Met. I may also visit the collection put together in a New York townhouse by the late financier Robert Lehman, and now housed in a building the Met put up to satisfy his demands. (That building even includes rooms from the townhouse.) And, if I look out the right window of the Met, I can see a marble wall of the Bank of the United States, built 1822 to '24, and transported, as in a dream, some years ago, to be implanted in a wall of the Met.

Central Park. The work of Frederick Law Olmsted and Calvert Vaux, talented, humane men. Of this precious stretch of ground, Olmsted wrote before the park was created well over a century ago: "The main object and justification is simply to produce a certain influence in the minds of people and through this to make life in the city healthier and happier. The character of this influence is a poetic one and it is to be produced by means of scenes, through observation of which the mind may be more or less lifted out of moods and habits into which it is, under the ordinary conditions of life in the city, likely to fall." Olmsted's ideal was uplifting, Victorian, sedate, essentially static. People would walk, sheep would graze. There would be a romantic castle to look at (the notion of building fake ruins still had not died out), gazebos to sit in. Peace.

It did not, in the end, work out that way. The sheep are gone and on the Sheep Meadow people fly kites, play touch football, throw Frisbees, stage protests of one kind or another. Elsewhere in the park, they play volleyball or softball and go to the Shakespeare Theatre (free) for which Joseph Papp, a consummate theatre man and politician, fought for so many years. (Better, far better that, than the proposal of one politician who, years after the park came into existence, proposed to make housing projects of it.) Sedate people still play at bowls in the park and others play tennis and on the weekends its curving roads are closed to automobile traffic and the bicyclers come out by the hundreds. Once, when it was safe to do so, New Yorkers slept in the park at night in the summertime. They do so no longer. There are times when it is not safe to walk through the park in the daytime. But, above all, it is the most used piece of parkland in the world and Olmsted and Vaux would, with reservations, have applauded it.

How else are the pressures to be relieved? Well, for one thing, music. There is the *grand luxe* music of the concert halls, of course, of Lincoln Center and of Carnegie Hall. But they are by no means all the music in New York. Beginning about the early Seventies or so, the city experienced a proliferation of music on the streets unequaled since the German and Italian brass bands disappeared and Fiorello LaGuardia threw the hurdy gurdys and the monkeys off the streets.

The new phenomenon is infinitely more sophisticated. One does not have to walk very far to hear a steel band, its musicians mostly the Caribbean people who have come to New York. They are a stirring, lively lot. And then, there are chamber-music ensembles. Incredible. More often than not, the members of these ensembles are conservatory graduates, and, often as not, they make as much as $200 of an afternoon or evening playing Scarlatti, Purcell, Telemann, and equally *recherché* things on the dusty sidewalks of Fifth Avenue or Greenwich Village. (I am reminded, acutely, of an old New York joke: "How do I get to Carnegie Hall?" Answer: "Practice!")

If music is not enough, there are mimes in the streets these days, their faces painted chalk-white, their lips red. And magicians. Obviously, they are learning their trade because they drop a lot of balls and fluttering doves have a habit of escaping before they are meant to. The streets teem with things now: Books are sold on the street, on Fifth Avenue, at the beginning of Central Park. Jewelry, sometimes the real thing, sometimes mass-produced fakes, is sold on both Fifth Avenue and on Eighth Street in Greenwich Village. And clothing. And food. I sometimes get the feeling when I see all these things that I have somehow been taken back to 18th-century Paris or London.

I have said nothing about the great New York Public Library. It has fallen on hard times, like so many things in New York, but it is still the finest general reference library in the world. For two reasons: It has the books and they are available to the public. That public is served by librarians who are miserably underpaid and yet devoted to learning with a ferocity I have seldom seen matched. It is impossible to count the number of grateful authors who, in the preface to their books (best-sellers and obscure scholarly works alike) have not failed to acknowledge the infinitely patient help of those who work for The New York Public Library.

I cannot exhaust the number of things a New Yorker can do to mitigate the pressures on him. But I can tell of one which never fails me. When, now and then, I find things getting to be too much for me, I walk over to the Morton Street pier on the Hudson River in Greenwich Village. The pier hasn't been used for shipping for years. (There are more than 400 miles of New York waterfront, and, as fewer and fewer ships come into it, more and more piers are abandoned and many of them burn down.) It has been turned into a kind of waterfront park and a lot of people go there to sit, to talk, to ride bicycles, to walk their dogs, to kiss or squabble, to get a tan or display their muscles and, for a while, to treat one another in a peaceful, neighborly fashion.

I like the place best in the late afternoon, when the sun is getting ready to drop back of New Jersey. Then, I sit on a steel bollard and look out across the water. The Statue of Liberty is barely to be seen in the haze down the Harbor. The water is filthy, but the sun gives it an unexpectedly beautiful texture. There is not nearly as much shipping to see as there once was, but there are the Circle Line boats going around Manhattan and the guide takes note of us; and there are people in small boats who hail us; and the noise of the city seems to subside.

The conversations about me are pitched low; for some reason, family quarrels, lovers' quarrels seem not to be conducted on the Morton Street pier. Occasionally, a gull flies by, looks inquisitively at the water for some piece of marine garbage he can eat, and flies away yelling either in triumph or disappointment. I never can tell which. And I don't much care. Because like the rest of the people on the pier I am rested, at peace, my mind filled for a change with lofty thoughts.

Preceding page: The surest sign of fall dying and winter coming in New York is neither the calendar nor the weather. It is the Macy's Thanksgiving Day Parade, a gorgeous jumble of balloons, cartoon figures, singers, dancers and bands.

We see here the interior of the Guggenheim
Museum on upper Fifth Avenue, only a short
distance from the Metropolitan. It is the only
monument by Frank Lloyd Wright in New York.
Wright detested the city, but he did let himself be
persuaded to take the money to build this museum.

The Metropolitan is the *grande dame* of museums in New York, one of the richest in the world, and in the opinion of many, a perfect exemplar of what an agglomeration of money, politics and taste can do to create a great institution where it is possible to reflect on a suit of armor or copy a portrait.

Visitors throng to the
Museum of Modern Art for
timely exhibitions and a look
at the always satisfying
permanent collection. Here,
from the staggering assembly
of 20th-century art are:

a Matisse paper cut-out
through the doorway, and a
Kupka color abstraction on
the near wall;

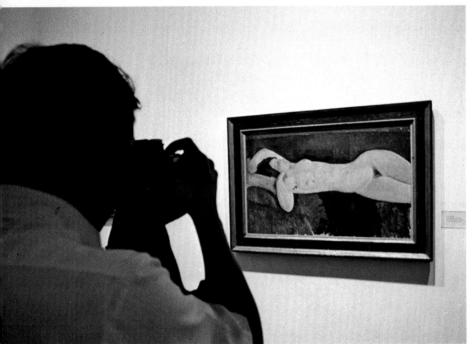

an elegantly elongated
Modigliani nude;

a Lehmbruck sculpture and a
pair of early Kokoschkas;

at right, Picasso's landmark
work *Les Demoiselles
d'Avignon*.

Not all of New York's art is displayed in museums.
This is a quiet street in Greenwich Village. Village
dwellers make strenuous efforts to preserve their
neighborhoods and what we are seeing here is a part
of a block association fair held once a year to raise
money. The art displayed is mostly that of Sunday
painters: if it sells, fine. If it does not, oh well.

Left: this is no Oriental bazaar, no North African casbah. It is only the northwest corner of Houston Street and West Broadway at the southern end of Greenwich Village which is, in reality, the northern end of Little Italy.

And, at the right, elsewhere in the neighborhood, Greek Revival houses from the 1830s and one of the wonderful Renaissance firehouses put up toward the end of the 19th century.

Henry James wrote of
Washington Square
(preceding page) that it had
"a kind of established repose
which is not of frequent
occurrence in other quarters
of the long, shrill city...." It
did once. Now, it does not.
Mothers still bring their
children to its small
playground in the daytime,
and people throw Frisbees,
but it is also full of derelicts
and trouble at night.

At the left is my mailman
in Greenwich Village, Frank
Schimler, a decent, diligent
man. He rests only
occasionally in a long day.
The dry cleaner at the right
takes his ease for a few
minutes on a bench
conveniently placed in his
shop doorway. Village
tradesmen and shopkeepers,
whose businesses sometimes
flow out onto the sidewalks
(below), keep neighborhood
streets busy—and safe.

Food of all nations is served at a block association fair in Greenwich Village.

Chess in Washington Square.

Before a surrealistic parade of good Italian breads, the good Italian baker takes a breather away from the heat of his ovens.

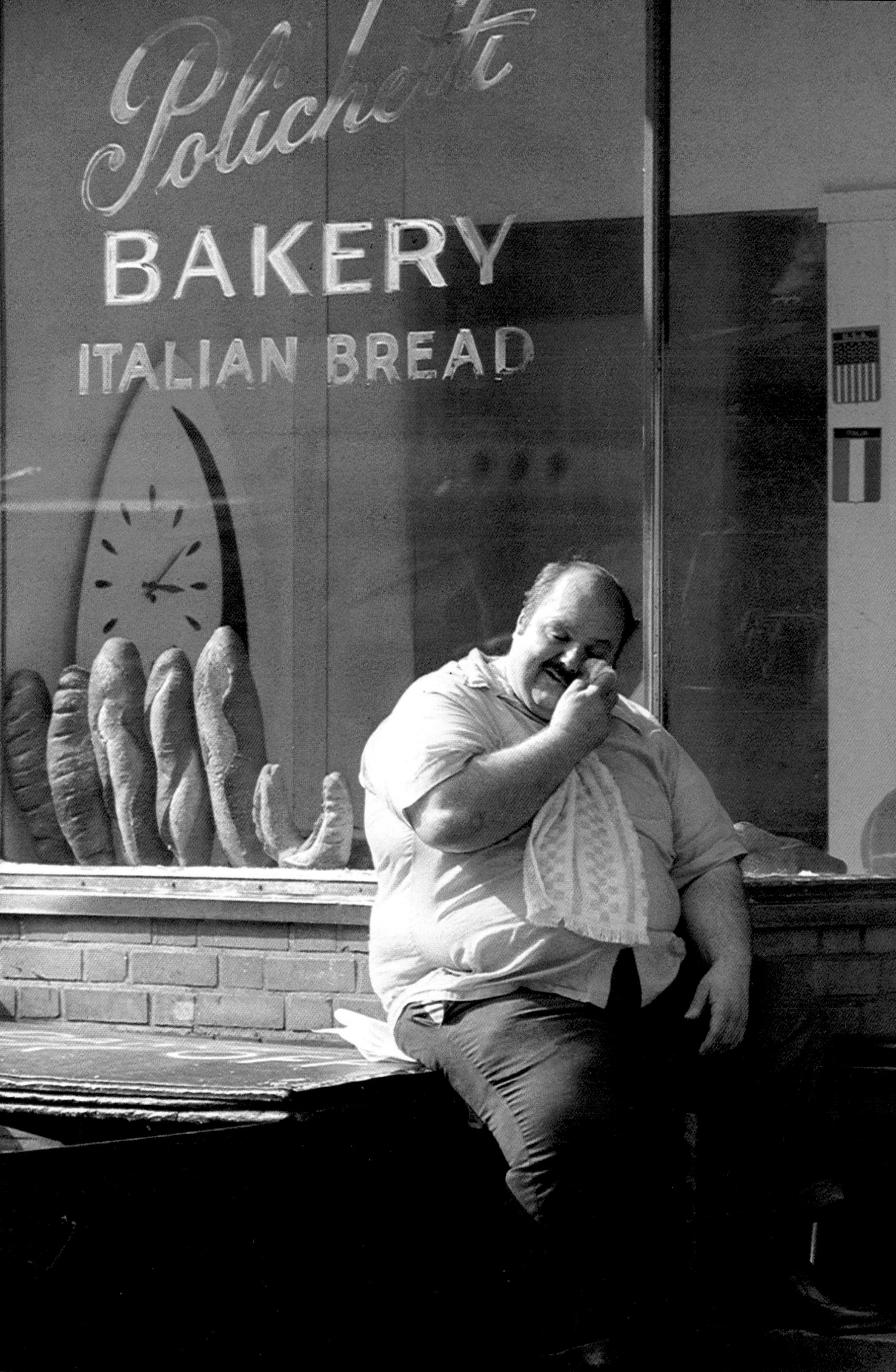
BAKERY
ITALIAN BREAD

Preceding page: Central
Park—the Bethesda
Fountain, created for the
strolls of proper Victorian
ladies and their escorts.
Today, it is no less a meeting
place.

How vast an expanse Central
Park is may be judged from
the photograph, above right,
taken from a building on the
Park's southern edge.
What to do in Central Park?
Almost anything, including
carriage rides, football, and
volleyball.

Preceding page: bicycle riding, without automobile traffic to interfere, on weekends.

The band shell near Bethesda Fountain often echoes to classical music, a rock band or the rhythms of a dance performance. But music needs no formal setting in Central Park: at left, a percussion trio with a steel drummer plays under an ancient maple; at right, a Latin group complete with conga drums, maracas, cowbell and an improvised beer-can instrument.

Overleaf: Fall color shimmers in the Park lake, reflecting *(left)* the roof of the American Museum of Natural History and a Central Park West apartment building.

HARLEM

MURAL DESIGN
AND
PROJECT DIRECTOR
NORMAN MESSIAH

ASSISTANT ARTISTS
MR. JAMES BUCKLEY
MR. THIEREY KUHN

The United States Bureau of the Census tells me that in 1960 the population of New York City was divided in this way: White, 78 per cent; Black, 13 per cent; Puerto Rican, 8 per cent; Others, 1 per cent. Then, it tells me that in 1975 the division was this: White, 62 per cent; Black, 22 per cent; Puerto Rican, 12 per cent; Others, 4 per cent. In the five years between 1970 and 1975, the city lost 600,000 whites. I am informed by the Bureau's figures that in 1975 the Borough of the Bronx became the first in the city's history whose blacks, Puerto Ricans, and "others" outnumbered the whites, 56 per cent to 44 per cent. In Manhattan, the white population dropped, in that fifteen-year period from 63 per cent to 58 per cent; the number of blacks, Puerto Ricans and again, "others," as they are known in the bureau's cabalistic numbers, rose from 37 per cent to 42 per cent.

I fix on Manhattan because it contains Harlem and Harlem is the runic word for black in New York, and, more recently, for the Hispanic. It is neither the first of the black settlements nor of the Hispanic in the city by a long shot; those go back up to two hundred years and more. Nor is it even the largest now. The South Bronx far exceeds it in population, devastation, and in crime and degradation. But no black or Hispanic section of the city equals it as the very symbol of the aspirations and the accomplishments of these people.

Until just before our entry into the First World War, Harlem was white—all white—a residential community for the upper middle class. (Richard Rodgers, the composer, was born in Harlem, for example—in a brownstone house at a corner of 116th Street and Fifth Avenue, where the avenue is interrupted by Mount Morris Park.) The developers of the late 19th and early 20th centuries saw, as expertly as any demographer of today with his computers, the direction in which the middle class might go as the tide of immigrants pushed it north and the city, perforce, had to expand. And, like all speculators, they overborrowed, they overbuilt, they oversold. What they left behind was long block after block of Italianate brownstones and big apartment houses and even such odd experiments as that undertaken by Stanford White and a few other noted architects: an entire block, with inner courtyard, of attached Romanesque homes. When Harlem became black and Hispanic, those homes came to be occupied by the rising black middle class and called, ironically, "Strivers' Row," the name it has today.

First, the banks told the speculators, "No more." Then the land fell in value and so did the buildings. And the middle class began to have misgivings, or make more money; in any case, it began to move elsewhere. And then, the First World War came along, and, with it, the migration northward of millions of blacks. In New York, they lived where they could and where they could live then, relatively cheaply, was Harlem. By the late twenties, Harlem was black, with a sprinkling of Spanish (many more would come later from Puerto Rico); the Irish were driven out of their pockets; the Italians held on much longer in East Harlem (some are still there, but in nothing like the numbers they used to be); and the most famous ghetto in the United States had been created.

I think I can best tell the way New York felt and feels about Harlem in an elliptical way, in which time is telescoped and attitude becomes all. In the Twenties, there occurred the Harlem Renaissance, the marvelous burgeoning of Negro (not black) culture, writing and composing and dancing and entertainment and fashion, a ferment which fully matched that of, say, Greenwich Village, although it was never as highly publicized. Carl Van Vechten, the novelist, celebrated it in a tender, catty novel called (attend the title, please!) "Nigger Heaven." And it was fashionable for whites to come up from downtown to the Negro speakeasies and nightclubs (run by white gangsters), to the Cotton Club and Connie's Inn and many, many other places, after 2 o'clock in the morning to enjoy themselves in a rather condescending way. For them Harlem was exotic, or bizarre, or "different."

Even during the depression that state of mind existed. My earliest experiences of Harlem are these: rent parties during the depression. One paid half a dollar, a dollar— not easily come by—and could eat and be entertained most of the night. The rent got paid. Saturday mornings, when it cost only a quarter, I sat in the balcony of the Apollo Theatre on 125th Street (owned by a white man) and saw the finest Negro talent in existence—fully the equal of anything to be seen at the Palace downtown—singers, dancers, orchestras, comedians.

I was exalted by such frivolous things as a tiny, frenetic man named Lucky Millinder standing in front of an orchestra called Mills Blue Rhythm Band and shouting a song called "Ride Red Ride." I was made hilarious by the sly comedy of a man named Dewey (Pigmeat) Markham. To this day, I believe it was from performers like Pigmeat that performers like Redd Foxx learned their timing, their delivery, and, yes, some of their lines. What the Apollo gave me was the last days of "coon humor," the kind of humor created by blacks *for* blacks, a tasty dish of self-deprecation, barely concealed outrage, and genuine humor.

Later, I danced at the Savoy Ballroom (torn down now) with Ella Fitzgerald. The Savoy was known then as "The Home of Happy Feet." Miss Fitzgerald was the singer with Chick Webb's band. The superb little hunchbacked drummer hired her after she won the Wednesday-night amateur contest at the Apollo. She was young and slim then, obliging, too, and would come down from the bandstand between sets and dance with outlanders like me. The dancing at the Savoy—Trucking and the Lindy Hop—was as spectacular as anything I have ever seen in my life. It was so powerful and so rhythmic and so heavy that new steel girders had to be built under the floor to keep it from collapsing.

That sort of thing ended not too long after the Second World War. For, even in the best of times for Harlem, poverty was unbelievable. The going uptown stopped. People grew uneasy about crime.

Harlem tries its damnedest to live. It fights for its schools and its churches (African Methodist Episcopal or Spanish storefront Pentecostal), its libraries and playgrounds, its decaying buildings, its many, many institutions. It fights against the crime eating it and the rot pervading it. And it fights, with indifferent success, the neglect of banks, government and the rest of the white world. And it doesn't like welfare any better than anybody else. And it exists.

But, if you are to know *how* it exists, you must listen to its voices. Hear the voice of Lawrence Jones, 14 and black, father gone, mother working in the post office, a slum boy. "I'm proud of my African heritage and all," he says, but he also says, "It's hard to be the blackest one in the family. Like they can only see me at night when I *smile.*" And, "Unless you're black, you can't really understand. Like the gangs and how you have to fight all the time. I have to get up at 4 in the morning to walk my mother to the subway just to make sure no one rips her off or mugs her. I was in class and the teacher was talking about how blacks are becoming more civilized.

"That's what he said. Civilized. Said that before, when we were slaves, we didn't know how to behave, but we're learning, the doors are opening up for us. I told him the doors weren't so open and we did know how to behave. He said he didn't want to discuss it. I told him he *had* to. I stood up and I guess he thought I was going to kick his ass. I felt like it. But he sent a kid for the principal. And the principal told me to try and be cool, relax, stay out of his way. When I grow up, I want to be a cop. Or a politician. Like if I were a cop, I could be fair and rap to the kids before I busted them. I could bust the pushers easy but be cool with the kids. Help them by telling them where it's at. If I was a politician, I'd change the laws and help the poor people. How come poor people have to live the way they do? 'Cause they're black, that's why. But . . . but . . . I don't really understand it. Just because you're black."

Hear Steve Rodriguez, 15, Puerto Rican. On his back, a sequined denim jacket and red stripes down the sides of his trousers. Combat boots with high heels. A safari hat. A costume. He's messed with cocaine, heroin, LSD, ups, downs. He draws. Graffiti. "Check it out, man. It's like leaving your mark. Like people know you're there. Me, CONAN, everywhere. In the school, on the building, in the train, in all the bathrooms. Only a few dudes in more places than I am. Dudes stop me in the streets and say, 'I saw yours at such and such.' And they dig it. They respect it because it's good. Sure, I got busted once. On the subway. So what. I got to stay out of the train yards now because they got dogs. Can you dig it? Dogs!

"I used to run with a gang. Sure. The Savage Skulls. I once had a piece—a gun. I messed up a lot of dudes and even got messed up myself. I killed one cat, shot him from a roof. I feel bad about that. Like I'll have to pay for it some time. No more piece. I studied the martial arts and I can dig it's cooler to run—fight by not fighting. Now, I know where it's at. A lot of dudes in this city don't know what's happening and they have to bust heads to let you know how *bad* they are. They ain't bad at all. Try and tell them that. I'd rather be in my room with my timbales. I know it's not cool to get high, but how do you think I really got into music? When I was high. Blow a little *chiba* or take a snort and I play all kinds of music. Rock, jazz, especially *mi latino.* I also found my philosophy when I was high, like I have this dialogue with myself and I understand God. It all comes to one place. Like we're all brothers. There's a *unity* man!"

And, finally, there is Luisa Perez, 32, Puerto Rican, black-haired, handsome, modest, mother of a 12-year-old son forever in trouble at school. Her husband left her, she works in a bank as a loan officer. She is admired and promoted by her white employers and she is especially valuable because she speaks two languages. But, she says, "I am not an American. Whites are Americans. I am Puerto Rican."

For me, that is the last irony. Because not only is Puerto Rico a commonwealth of the United States and its people citizens at birth, but Louisa Perez was born on the mainland, in New York City, not even in Puerto Rico. That is how far estrangement is sometimes carried in Harlem.

Harlem is blocks and blocks of important-looking Italianate apartment buildings bordering Morningside Park (*left.*)

And street after street of three- and four-story dwellings, fronted with brownstone taken from the huge deposits in Connecticut. Being soft, the stone was easily carved and ornamented, and, being soft, it sometimes crumbles. Crumbled, patched, or brightly-painted to mask its scars, the Harlem brownstone still stands.

The life of Harlem is hard but even the police smile
now and then. Open-fronted shops tumble out onto
the sidewalks on 125th Street and nearby,
resembling the markets of the Old World. And
overhead, in the din of steel wheels on steel tracks,
the suburbanites ride through this city-within-a-city
that is Harlem.

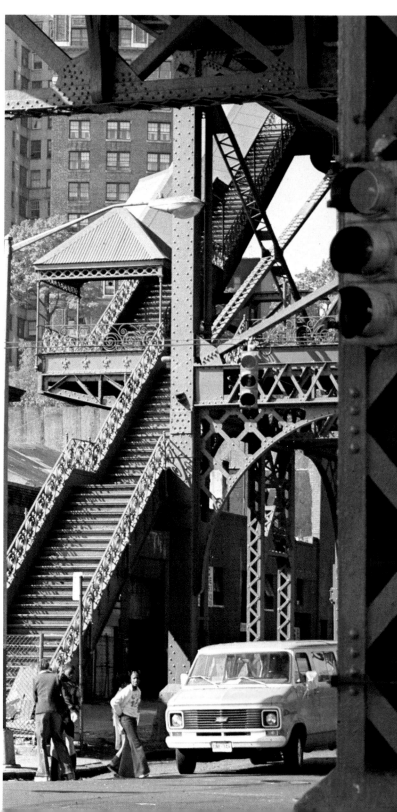

Harlem's markets are set up chock-a-block under
the forbidding viaduct of the railroad along Park
Avenue in East Harlem.

Overleaf: a panoramic view of Harlem made from
the top of the new New York State Office Building,
built to spread some of the city's jobs and
development into the ghetto.

The panorama *(preceding page)* provides a falsely serene look. On the ground, there is something else: Buildings are abandoned; they burn and are torn down. The empty lots fill with rubble and garbage. Life on this battleground is no joke.

It is difficult to credit it, but children still dance in a
Harlem schoolyard. An artist will sketch. And its
streets are sometimes dangerous, but always alive.

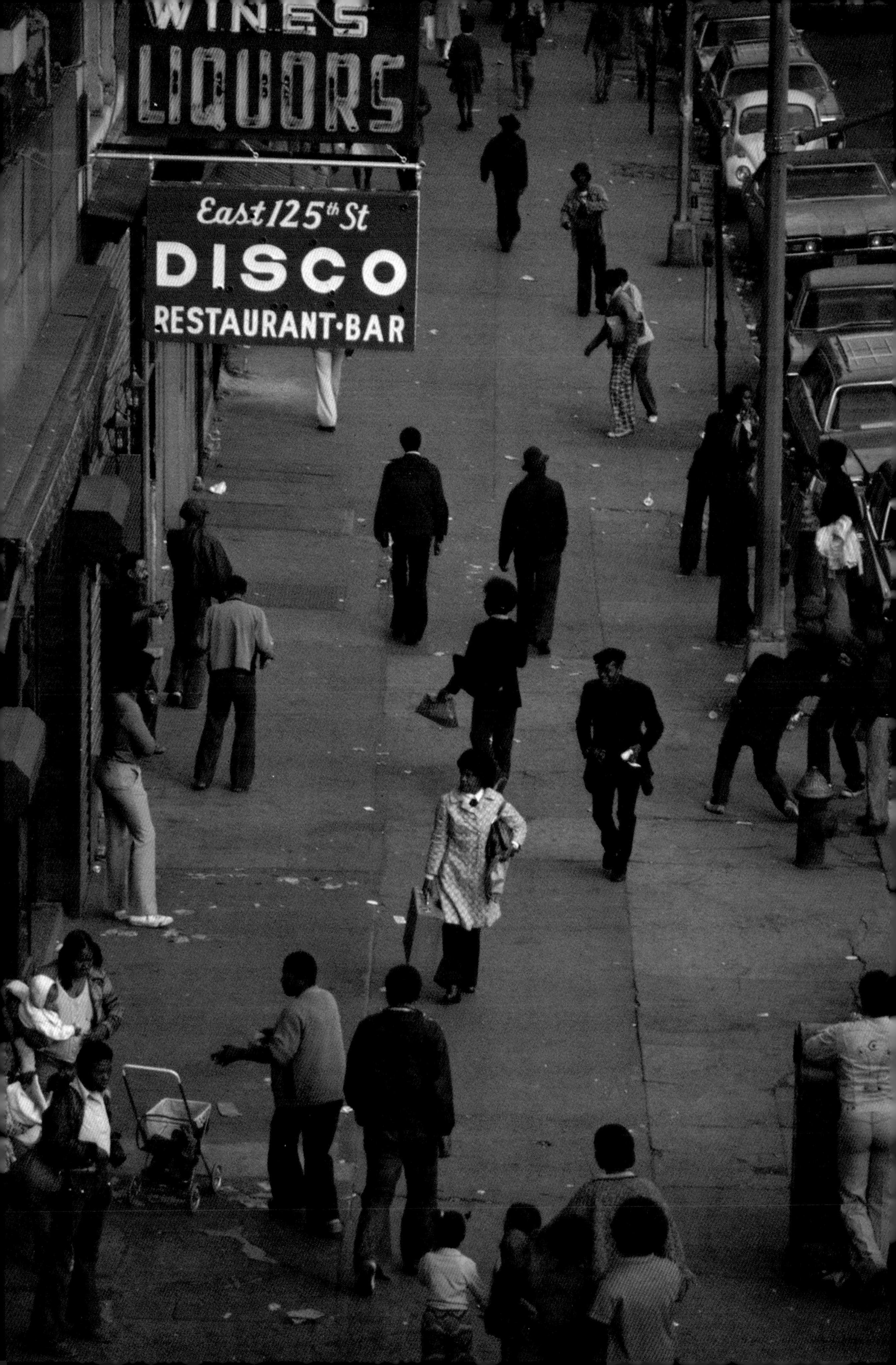
WINES
LIQUORS
East 125th St
DISCO
RESTAURANT·BAR

Children everywhere love sports, but the motivation to excel in the ghetto is especially strong; the good athlete can play his way out of the slums.

A playground on 139th Street.

Football at 128th Street and Third Avenue.

Basketball before a crude, but spectacular mural.

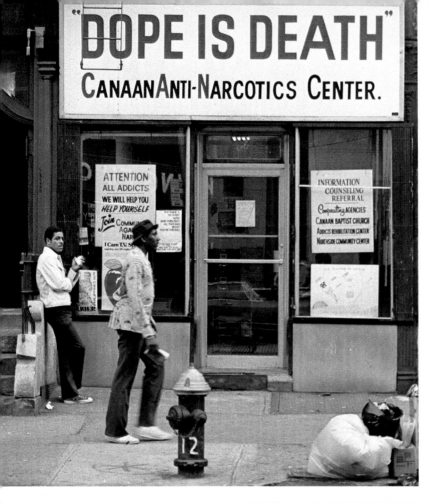

In Harlem, as in other poor parts of the city, there is junk. Smack. Heroin. Ups and Downs. Grass. *Chiba*. You name it, they've got it. Right out in the open. A supermarket of junk on the corners of 116th Street and Eighth Avenue.

Harlem is full of the voices crying for liberation. They are the trumpeting of a politician with his portable public-address system, the quiet invitation of a bookstore selling only books about blacks by blacks.
They are also a speech in the Temple of Liberation. And decals bespeaking African pride above the license plate of an automobile.

Overleaf: the muralist's art has had a new revival in the ghetto—the inheritance of Rivera, Siqueiros, Orozco and the protest artists of the 1930s. Here, the aims and aspirations of the city are laid out in bold forms and colors.

Here is the Black Muslim temple on 116th Street and *(below)* a service. The Black Muslims have changed since the revolutionary days of the 1960s; they have given up a good many of the businesses they started; they have given up hating whites; they have withdrawn, more and more, into their religion.

Many beliefs and styles of religion flourish in Harlem. This is the Canaan Baptist Church on East 116th Street. Chorus. Sermon. Baptism.

And, on the following page, the splendid Mount Olivet Church at 120th Street and Lenox Avenue. It is a Sunday morning. Mount Olivet is the richest church in Harlem.

I have always found the famous poem of Emma Lazarus, fixed first on a tablet on the pedestal of the Statue of Liberty, and now to be found, as well, at the immigration station at Kennedy International Airport, to be well-meaning but a little too mawkish for my taste, not to say somewhat condescending. We know it well: "Give me your tired, your poor,/Your huddled masses yearning to breathe free,/The wretched refuse of your teeming shore./ Send these, the homeless, tempest-tost to me,/I lift my lamp beside the golden door!" But what else could have been expected of this bluestocking spinster, do-gooder, daughter of wealthy parents of Portuguese-Jewish descent, this acquaintance of the rarefied Emerson circle in Concord, Massachusetts?

For me, the poetry of immigration, of the melting pot, is in something quite different and I found it, a few years ago, in the subway, on the windows near the doors. It reads: *"AVISO. La vía del tren subterraneo es peligrosa."* Enchanting. And : *"Si el tren se para entre las estaciones quédese adentro."* Foreboding. And: *"NO SALGA AFUERA."* Far places? And: *"Siga las instrucciones de los operadores del tren o la policía."* Some sort of description of the leader of millions of wanderers?

None of these things. For those who, like myself, do not read Spanish, there is a companion notice in English: "WARNING. Subway tracks are dangerous. If the train stops between stations stay inside. Do not get out. Follow instructions of train crews or police." I choose to ignore the notice in English and to insist, stubbornly, to myself that the liquid syllables, the delicious sibilants I see in Spanish are, in fact, the highest poetry of the melting pot. And, in a manner of speaking, they are, telling travelers in noble but practical Castilian what to do in the event of an emergency.

It is commonly supposed that, apart from the Indians, the earliest settlers of Manhattan were the Dutch. That is not quite the case. The Dutch East India Company, which supervised things for the monarchy, was no less xenophobic than any such organization and one of its stipulations was that all settlers must speak Dutch and Low Dutch at that. Yet, among those first settlers under the Dutch were no fewer than eighteen nationalities, including Swedes and Norwegians, Frenchmen, Belgians, Italians, Turks, Spaniards, Germans and Finns. And, before the English finally got New Amsterdam (once by conquest, once by treaty) most of those names were Dutchified and we have learned, only in recent years, that they weren't Dutch at all. Thus, Sarah Rapelie, a Walloon, becomes Rapelje, and Guillaume Vigne, a Frenchman, becomes Willem Vinge.

Another note on the Dutch, this one concerning the Jews. When we think of the Jews in New York, we tend to think of the 2,000,000 who fled the Pale of Czarist Russia and the Austro-Hungarian empire between the assassination of Alexander II and the First World War. But, there was a Dutch Jew in New York, in July, 1654. And, a month later, twenty-three more—men, women and children—refugees then, as afterward. These were the descendants of Jews expelled from Spain and Portugal during the Inquisition in 1492. They settled first, some of them, in Holland, and then in Brazil, after the Dutch took part of that country. When the Portuguese threw the Dutch out of Brazil, this intrepid group of Jews took flight once more, this time on a Dutch ship bound for Holland. The vessel was intercepted by a Spanish warship which, in turn, was attacked by a French privateer. The Jews were taken aboard the French ship and landed in New York. Peter Stuyvesant, the governor, did not want them at all. He requested of the Dutch East India Company, that "none of the Jewish nation be permitted to infest New Netherland." He was summarily overruled and the Jews were permitted to stay, providing they did not become public charges—which they did not.

There is literally no race on earth, no nationality, which has not inhabited New York at one time or another. It is a commonplace that the Italians built the subways and dug the ditches; that the Irish fled the potato famines in the old country to become policemen and politicians in New York; that the Germans and French ran the restaurants. But it is also true that tens of thousands of Scottish and Irish and German and Jewish stone carvers came to this country from 1850 on because there was building going on and ornament required to be carved on those buildings. Some of those buildings were poorly built tenements and the carving on them was simply to dress them up for ignorant immigrants who thought they were getting something better than they were. And some of those buildings were put up for their middle- and upper-class betters in limestone and granite and marble. The stone carvers were dour men, heavy drinkers, and, more often than not, bachelors. They worked hard, contracted lung diseases, lived lives of depressing anonymity (hardly any of their work is signed) and died young. But they left thousands of their marks—faces and masks and cartouches and grotesque images—on buildings still standing. When the style in architecture changed and ornament fell out of favor, the stone carvers, too, disappeared. There are only a few left—a handful of old men, a handful of young men, their descendants, attempting to learn the craft.

The greatest period of immigration this or any other country has ever known took place between the opening of Ellis Island in 1892 and the beginning of the first World War. The island and its red-brick and limestone-trim buildings was closed in 1954 and then, quite properly, declared a historic monument and reopened as a park and museum in the spring of 1976. Between the time Ellis Island opened and the day it closed, 12,000,000 people came through it to enter the United States. It is estimated that there are a hundred million living Americans whose ancestors were processed through that dismal funnel out in New York Harbor. Now, whatever immigrants there are enter New York in other ways—through the airports, mainly, or through Canada, Mexico or the West Coast.

The relics of all those millions of old immigrants and those who followed them are everywhere around New York. In the food, on the signs, in the clothing, in the habits of long standing. When I see rude paintings on the walls of loft buildings in Lower Manhattan or in Harlem, I know they are the work of either immigrant artists or the children of immigrant artists. (Remember, the Puerto Ricans, who paint so many of these buildings, consider themselves to be immigrants.)

I know that the festival of San Gennaro on Mulberry Street, with the gilded statue of the saint carried in procession every September, is the direct descendant of the same thing in Sorrento or Sicily or Salerno or wherever in Italy. Thousands upon thousands of Jews have left the city, but they seem all to come back every Sunday to shop on Orchard Street. So many, that the street is closed to traffic on that day.

Do you want to see the descendants of immigrants elsewhere? Then go to the parades on Fifth Avenue—the whirling, brilliant Puerto Rico Day observance; the Polish Pulaski Day parade; the St. Patrick's Day parade for the Irish. Each is distinct; each tells of its own heritage. And each bespeaks the influence of the melting pot on them. How? Quite simply. All the marching bands, at one point or another, play "The Stars and Stripes Forever."

The grave-looking gentlemen in fur hats and long black coats are Hasidic Jews in Williamsburg, Brooklyn.

Jews (not just Hasidim) poured out of the Lower East Side of Manhattan after 1897, when the Williamsburg Bridge was opened. They poured into Williamsburg in such numbers that the bridge came to be known as ''The Jews' Highway.''

Many hundreds of thousands of Jews are gone now, both from Williamsburg and the Lower East Side, but there is a wall mural on the East Side to mark the great immigration. And Hasidic children still living in Williamsburg. And Jewish merchants on Orchard Street in Manhattan.

For Orchard Street, the great day of the week is Sunday. It is then that traffic is stopped in the street and thousands of people come to buy, to bargain and to jostle peacefully.

Jews come to Orchard Street not just to buy but to try to bring to life the stories their parents and grandparents told them about life on the East Side.

And, if they can find time between bargaining and buying, they may also see Jewish devouts on the streets who have higher things to think about than drygoods.

There are more Puerto Ricans, Hispanics and Blacks now on the Lower East Side than there are Jews. They live in the tenements from which the Jews fled when they could. They are proud of their heritage—some of them—and boast of it on flags. And they take their diversions peacefully—some of them—playing dominoes on the sidewalk.

Overleaf: the muralist's art flourishes also on the Lower East Side, that other, older ghetto. If one cannot *have* what one wants or needs, it can be expressed cheaply enough, and often quite adroitly, in paint.

There are thousands of Haitians in New York now. One of their great, native traditions is group dancing, as demonstrated here at a "One World Festival."

Here, in a Brooklyn basement, is a Haitian voodoo ceremony. The *hougan*, or voodoo priest, has invoked the spirits. The subject, at left, has entered his trance. We do not know where he is going; we do not know when he will be back.

The parades of New York speak for themselves; the bands and the pipers blare without restraint. The merchants of Fifth Avenue would rather do without them but New York would not be the same without its parades.

In Chinatown and adjoining Little Italy (which has shrunk as Chinatown expanded), we may find the following:

This ancient standing in the doorway of a tenement built for immigrants of another race.

Telephone booths in the shape of pagodas, courtesy of the New York Telephone Company.

A Buddhist temple. The real thing. Not for tourists. Patronized mostly by Taiwanese living in New York.

And the old Italian musicians, equally ready to play for weddings, funerals and the festivals of San Gennaro, St. Anthony, Our Lady of Pompeii.

More Chinatown. Fruit and vegetables at Mulberry and Canal Streets.

And a pair of murals; the wall painting at Pike Street has a mysterious, surreal quality about it. The artist is superior to many others who cover the walls of buildings.

There is no race on earth that has not lived in New York at one time or another.

These are Hispanics. And this is *their* Fifth Avenue parade. Vivid. Whirling. Exotic.

September. The Festival of San Gennaro. Mulberry Street in Little Italy.

It is as sure to happen every year as the harvest of corn and wheat.

At San Gennaro, the harvest is money pinned to the image of the saint as he is paraded through the crowded streets to the squealing of clarinets, the grunting of tubas, the slam of drums and the warnings of trombones.

It is doubtful that any nationality in New York has not celebrated its presence in the city with a parade.

This one happens to be German—the Steuben Day parade, honoring the German general of the Revolution. But, no matter what the parade, or who is being honored, the Irish are omnipresent: these are players of the Emerald Society of Suffolk County, on Long Island.

One last thing. It sometimes seems that the most characteristic figure in any of these parades is neither the grand marshal, nor the drum major, nor the piper, nor veterans, nor the matrons of this or that auxiliary, but the lone, brave figure in the foreground of the photograph on the left.

He is the sanitation man. The man with the broom. The street sweeper. New York little notes nor long remembers his presence in a parade. But were he not there, Fifth Avenue would be filthy the next day and the rich, in their apartments lining the avenue, would scream to high heaven.

Overleaf: In ethnic dress, the dance goes on. New York, for all its problems, its bewildering racial diversity, its noise and dirt—for those who know it, is still the most exciting city on earth.